Miles goes to
ROME

A place-based story and activity
book for young explorers

by Lucy Barry
Art by Jec R.

puddle jump kids

First published in the United States in 2025
A production of Puddle Jump Kids, LLC
Connecticut, USA
www.puddlejumpkidsco.com

Written by Lucy Barry
Artwork by Jec R.
Edited by T. McBrien
and D. Mele

ISBN 979-8-218-86624-2

With special thanks to L, Q, & R

Hello there!

I'm Miles, and I love adventures. Today's adventure takes us to **Rome, Italy.**

Italy is a country in Europe. It's shaped like a boot!

Almost 60 million people live in Italy. Rome is Italy's biggest city. There are 4.3 million people in Rome.

That's enough people to fill 60 soccer stadiums!

Rome's birthday is April 21, in 753 BC.
It is almost 3,000 years old!

You can arrive in Rome by airplane, train, car, or bus. Today, I arrive by train!

Rome has a rich history, and
there is a lot to see and do.

Some of it is new,
and some of it is very old.

Let's check it out!

I start my day by walking through Campo de' Fiori. It is Rome's historic market.

I am sure to say "Buongiorno" to everyone I see.
This means "Hello!" in Italian.

My first stop is the Colosseum. It is the most visited and famous place in Rome. The Colosseum was built 2,000 years ago out of stone, concrete, and brick.

The Colosseum was very advanced for its time. It is shaped like an ellipse, so that the entire audience could see the arena floor. It even had a roof that could be taken on or off, depending on the weather.

We are used to seeing big stadiums in today's world, but back in Ancient Rome, the Colosseum was enormous! It could fit up to 80,000 people. Visitors would come to watch gladiator battles and other spectacles.

Nearby is the Roman Forum. This is where ancient Romans shopped and met up with friends. It's kind of like today's main streets, except that it existed thousands of years ago!

I am getting hungry, so I stop for gelato. Gelato is Italian ice cream, and it is so delicious. There are lots and lots of flavors. It's hard to pick! I choose three popular ones: hazelnut, pistachio, and stracciatella. Stracciatella is vanilla with ribbons of chocolate in it.

Stra-chee-ah-tell-ah, per favore!

Miles Wants to Know

What is your favorite flavor?

The shopkeeper tells me that the ice cream cone was invented in Italy! It turns out that lots of cool things were invented here. Eyeglasses, the espresso machine, thermometers, the piano, cologne, and the typewriter, just to name a few.

Opera was invented in Italy over four centuries ago, too. An opera is like a play, but the story is told through singing, music, and dance. Opera is enjoyed all over the world, and in lots of languages. Music, theater, and the arts are an important part of Italian culture.

Miles Wants to Know

What's your favorite
thing to draw or paint?

Italy is also famous for its paintings. In fact, there is a very famous Italian artist you may have heard of.

Michelangelo!

He painted beautiful scenes on the ceiling of a well-known church called the Sistine Chapel. He did this over 500 years ago, and it's still a masterpiece!

It must have been very hard to paint while looking up the whole time.

The Sistine Chapel is in a part of Rome called Vatican City — but it's not in Italy! Vatican City is actually its very own country. In fact, it's the smallest country in the world.

Imagine if your town had a whole country right in the middle of it.
If you lived in Rome, that would be Vatican City.

An important person lives here.
Have you ever heard of the Pope?

The Pope is the leader of the Catholic Church. Nearly 1.3 billion people in the world are Catholic. When someone becomes Pope, they stay Pope for the rest of their life.

Did You Know?

There have been more than 260 Popes throughout history.

Next, I go to the Trevi Fountain. Legend says that if you throw a coin into the fountain, you will return to Rome. Tossing two coins means you will return and fall in love. And tossing three coins? That means you will come back, fall in love, and get married!

Lots of people throw coins into the Trevi Fountain. Over a million dollars is collected each year and the money is used to help people in need.

I definitely want to come back, so I toss in a coin!

I continue walking, and I notice the letters SPQR carved into old stones. In Ancient Rome, this meant "The Senate and the People of Rome." In other words, "this belongs to Rome."

It's the Ancient Roman equivalent of putting a name tag on your stuff. Except that instead of just belonging to you, it belongs to the entire city!

There is so much to see in Rome! And guess what? There's even more underground!

Over a long, long time, new buildings and dirt have added many layers to the city. I never would have guessed it from the street, but there are still entire buildings from thousands of years ago underneath my paws!

Much of Rome's history was shaped by a man named Julius Caesar, who ruled the city over 2,000 years ago. He was the first person to lead the Roman Republic — kind of like a king or an emperor. Julius Caesar was considered the most powerful person in the world when he was alive.

Julius Caesar was so powerful, he even changed the way we measure time. He was responsible for creating the calendar year we use today. In fact, the month of July comes from the name "Julius" — it was chosen in his honor.

Did You Know?

The site where Julius Caesar died is now a cat sanctuary, where cats without homes can live amongst the ruins and are given shelter, food, and medicine! It is called Largo di Torre Argentina.

I make my way to the busy Piazza Navona. It's a wide, beautiful square with restaurants and shops. Lots of people come here in the evening. Tonight, there is a performer playing music for everyone by the fountain in the center. I love to dance!

Not far away is a cool-looking building called the Pantheon. It's super old – almost 2,000 years. And it's still standing today! The Pantheon has a giant round roof, called a dome. Right in the middle of the dome is a big round hole. Sunlight shines through it like a spotlight. Sometimes raindrops fall through, too, but luckily, the floor has tiny, hidden drains to carry the water away. Inside, the Pantheon feels huge!

After the Pantheon, I decide to do some shopping to remember my trip. There are so many food and clothing shops in Rome. I head to Via del Corso. It is a long street that runs straight through the center of the city. It has everything I could ever want to buy!

Wow, what a day! I must have walked 100 miles. Rome is wonderful to visit. I've worked up a big appetite, so I sit at an outdoor cafe and rest my paws. Italy has amazing food. My favorite is pasta al pomodoro. That means pasta with fresh tomato sauce!

Thank you for coming on this big adventure with me today! I have to run back to the train station now so I can get to my next stop.

Here are a few activities for you to keep the adventure going on your own!

See you soon,

Miles the Cat

ROME WITH MILES, A TO Z

A Ancient

B Basilica

C Colosseum

D Dome

E Emperors

F Fountain

G Gelato

H History

I Italy

ROME WITH MILES, A TO Z

J

Julius Caesar

K

Keys

L

Largo di Torre Argentina

M

Michelangelo

N

Navona

O

Opera

P

Pantheon

Q

Quirinale Palace

R

Rome

ROME WITH MILES, A TO Z

S

Sistine Chapel

T

Trevi Fountain

U

Underground

V

Vatican

W

Walking

XVI

Roman Numerals

Y Years

July

 **Z**

Zoo

FIND IT

Can you find all the items that were invented in Italy?

Piano   Coffee Machine   Typewriter   Thermometer   Eyeglasses

POP QUIZ

What is the name of the country that can be found inside Rome?

How many coins should you throw into the Trevi Fountain if you wish to come back to Rome?

What four letters are found carved on old walls and stones in Rome?

How many people can fit inside the Colosseum?

POP QUIZ

Which famous artist painted the ceiling of the Sistine Chapel?

How do you say 'hello' in Italian?

Which Ancient Roman person is responsible for the calendar we use today?

Name one item that was invented in Italy.

PACK YOUR BAG

Color or circle the items you would pack in your backpack on a trip to Rome!

JOURNAL IT

Write three words that come to mind when you think of visiting Rome.

....
....
....

What is the one thing that excites you most about Rome?

....
....
....
....

What places would you like to visit in Rome?

....

....

....

Draw them in the space below!

LANGUAGE LESSON

Practice the Italian words below.

Hello ~ Buongiorno
Bwon-jor-no

Goodbye ~ Ciao
Chow

Please ~ Per favore
Per fah-vore-ay

thank you ~ Grazie
Grat-see

Cat ~ Gatto
Got-toe

Dog ~ Cane
Kah-nay

Book ~ Libro
Lee-bro

Toys ~ Giocattoli
Joe-kuh-toe-lee

Park ~ Parco
Par-ko

Eat ~ Mangiare
man-jar-ay

Bathroom ~ Bagno
Bahn-yo

House ~ Casa
Kah-sah

Water ~ Acqua
Ah-kwah

Sun ~ Sole
Sow-leh

LANGUAGE LESSON

Now draw lines connecting the Italian words to the pictures.

Sole

Libro

Acqua

Gatto

Casa

TIME TO EAT

Decorate the pizza below with your favorite toppings!

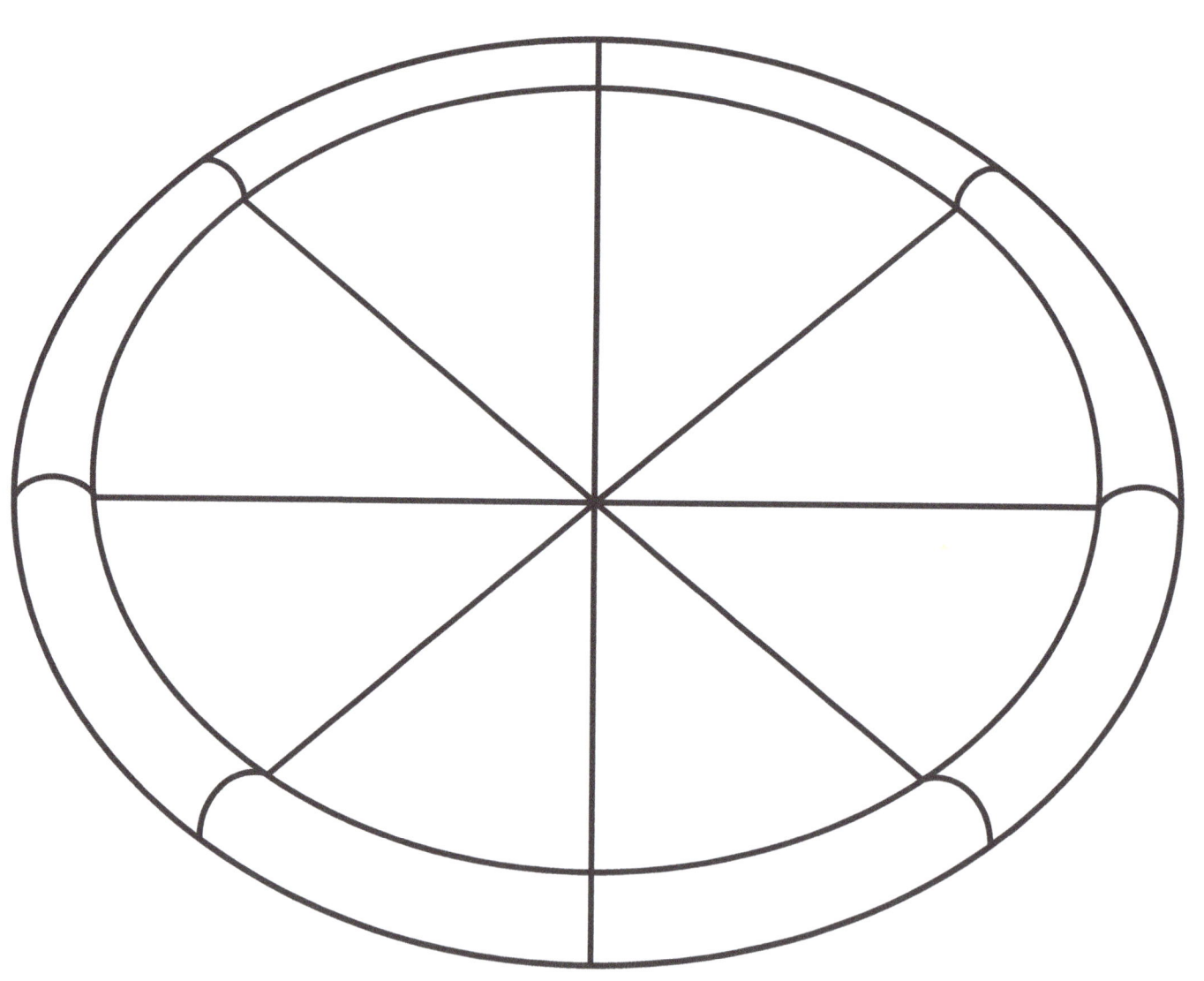

TIME TO EAT

Save room for dessert! Color the gelatos.

WHERE'S MILES?

Find and circle Miles!

TIC TAC TOURNEY

Grab a friend and face off to see who can win at tic tac toe!

Final Score:

X _____   O _____

COMPLETE THE MAZE

Find your way through the Colosseum!

START

FINISH

CONNECT THE DOTS

Do you recognize this famous Roman landmark?

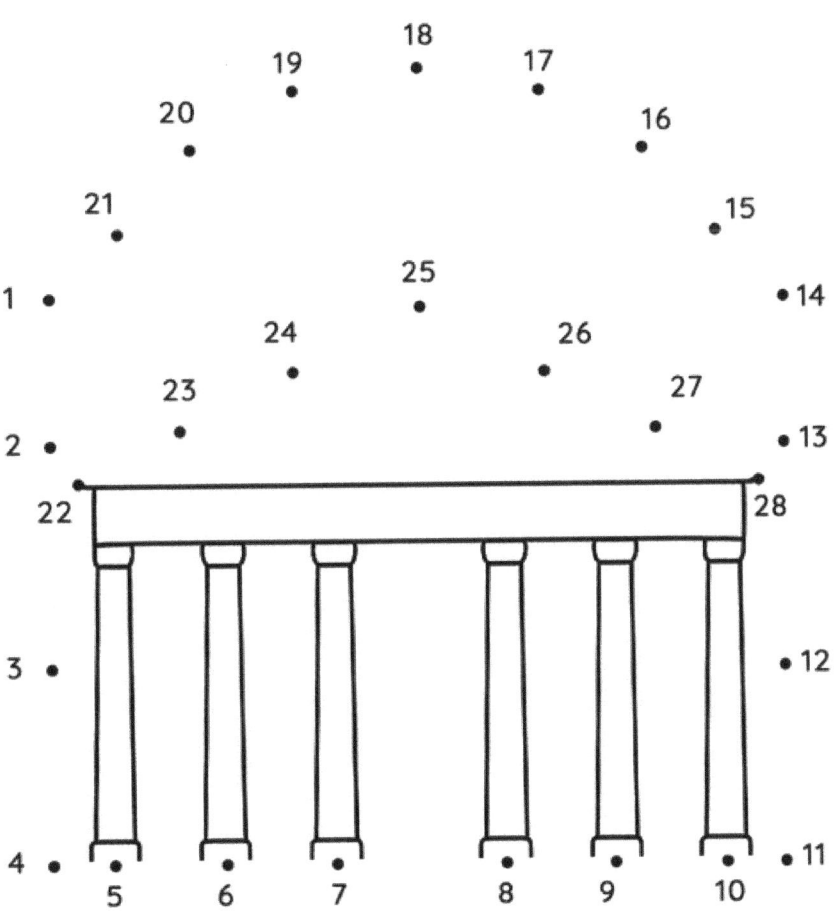

DESIGN A POSTCARD

Design a postcard from Rome...

DESIGN A POSTCARD

...and write a message to a friend about your trip!

WORD SEARCH

F	D	G	L	A	D	I	A	T	O	R	Q	R
V	A	T	I	C	A	N	C	I	T	Y	X	J
E	O	P	E	J	R	B	Q	D	A	F	H	F
O	P	E	R	A	T	C	A	F	A	R	T	I
S	T	R	A	C	C	I	A	T	E	L	L	A
A	V	T	T	R	E	V	I	S	P	N	C	S
U	N	D	E	R	G	R	O	U	N	D	A	P
C	A	F	E	G	L	O	I	A	T	O	F	Q
P	Z	Z	A	C	G	R	E	V	S	T	E	R

GLADIATOR   VATICAN CITY   OPERA
STRACCIATELLA   ART   TREVI   SPQR
UNDERGROUND   CAFÉ

PICTURE IT

Draw a picture of yourself in Rome!

ANSWER KEY

FIND IT

Can you find all the items items that were invented in Italy?

Piano   Coffee Machine   Typewriter   Thermometer   Eyeglasses

POP QUIZ

What is the name of the country that can be found inside Rome?

Vatican City

How many coins should you throw into the Trevi Fountain if you wish to come back to Rome?

One

What four letters are found engraved on walls and stones throughout Rome?

SPQR

How many people used to fit inside the Colosseum?

80,000

POP QUIZ

Who was the artist that painted the ceiling of the Sistine Chapel?

Michelangelo

How do you say hello in Italian?

Buongiorno

Which ancient Roman figure is responsible for the calendar we use today?

Julius Caesar

Name at least one item that was invented in Italy.

See page 12

LANGUAGE LESSON

Now draw a line connecting the Italian word to the corresponding picture.

Sole

Libro

Acqua

Gatto

Casa

WHERE'S MILES?

COMPLETE THE MAZE

Find your way through the Colosseum!

START

ANSWER KEY

CONNECT THE DOTS

Do you recognize this famous Roman landmark?

(it's the Pantheon!)

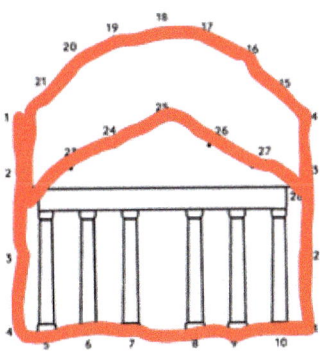

WORD SEARCH

GLADIATOR   VATICAN CITY   OPERA
STRACCIATELLA ART TREVI SPQR
UNDERGROUND CAFÉ